The Eldest Son by John Galsworthy

John Galsworthy was born at Kingston Upon Thames in Surrey, England, on August 14th 1867 to a wealthy and well established family. His schooling was at Harrow and New College, Oxford before training as a barrister and being called to the bar in 1890. However, Law was not attractive to him and he travelled abroad becoming great friends with the novelist Joseph Conrad, then a first mate on a sailing ship.

In 1895 Galsworthy began an affair with Ada Nemesis Pearson Cooper, the wife of his cousin Major Arthur Galsworthy. The affair was kept a secret for 10 years till she at last divorced and they married on 23rd September 1905.

Galsworthy first published in 1897 with a collection of short stories entitled "The Four Winds". For the next 7 years he published these and all works under his pen name John Sinjohn. It was only upon the death of his father and the publication of "The Island Pharisees" in 1904 that he published as John Galsworthy.

His first play, The Silver Box in 1906 was a success and was followed by "The Man of Property" later that same year and was the first in the Forsyte trilogy. Whilst today he is far more well know as a Nobel Prize winning novelist then he was considered a playwright dealing with social issues and the class system. Here we publish Villa Rubein, a very fine story that captures Galsworthy's unique narrative and take on life of the time.

He is now far better known for his novels, particularly The Forsyte Saga, his trilogy about the eponymous family of the same name. These books, as with many of his other works, deal with social class, upper-middle class lives in particular. Although always sympathetic to his characters, he reveals their insular, snobbish, and somewhat greedy attitudes and suffocating moral codes. He is now viewed as one of the first from the Edwardian era to challenge some of the ideals of society depicted in the literature of Victorian England.

In his writings he campaigns for a variety of causes, including prison reform, women's rights, animal welfare, and the opposition of censorship as well as a recurring theme of an unhappy marriage from the women's side. During World War I he worked in a hospital in France as an orderly after being passed over for military service.

He was appointed to the Order of Merit in 1929, after earlier turning down a knighthood, and awarded the Nobel Prize in 1932 though he was too ill to attend.

John Galsworthy died from a brain tumour at his London home, Grove Lodge, Hampstead on January 31st 1933. In accordance with his will he was cremated at Woking with his ashes then being scattered over the South Downs from an aeroplane.

Index of Contents

THE ELDEST SON

PERSONS OF THE PLAY

SIR WILLIAM CHESHIRE, a baronet
LADY CHESHIRE, his wife
BILL, their eldest son
HAROLD, their second son
RONALD KEITH (in the Lancers), their son-in-law
CHRISTINE (his wife), their eldest daughter
DOT, their second daughter
JOAN, their third daughter
MABEL LANFARNE, their guest
THE REVEREND JOHN LATTER, engaged to Joan
OLD STUDDENHAM, the head-keeper
FREDA STUDDENHAM, the lady's-maid
YOUNG DUNNING, the under-keeper
ROSE TAYLOR, a village girl
JACKSON, the butler
CHARLES, a footman

TIME: The present.

SCENE: The action passes on December 7 and 8 at the Cheshires' country house, in one of the shires.

ACT I

SCENE I

The scene is a well-lighted, and large, oak-panelled hall, with an air of being lived in, and a broad, oak staircase. The dining-room, drawing-room, billiard-room, all open into it; and under the staircase a door leads to the servants' quarters. In a huge fireplace a log fire is burning. There are tiger-skins on the floor, horns on the walls; and a writing-table against the wall opposite the fireplace. **FREDA STUDDENHAM**, a pretty, pale girl with dark eyes, in the black dress of a lady's-maid, is standing at the foot of the staircase with a bunch of white roses in one hand, and a bunch of yellow roses in the other. A door closes above, and **SIR WILLIAM CHESHIRE**, in evening dress, comes downstairs. He is perhaps fifty-eight, of strong build, rather bull-necked, with grey eyes, and a well-coloured face, whose choleric autocracy is veiled by a thin urbanity. He speaks before he reaches the bottom.

SIR WILLIAM
Well, Freda! Nice roses. Who are they for?

FREDA
My lady told me to give the yellow to Mrs. Keith, Sir William, and the white to Miss Lanfarne, for their first evening.

SIR WILLIAM
Capital.

[Passing on towards the drawing-room.

Your father coming up to-night?

FREDA
Yes.

SIR WILLIAM
Be good enough to tell him I specially want to see him here after dinner, will you?

FREDA
Yes, Sir William.

SIR WILLIAM
By the way, just ask him to bring the game-book in, if he's got it.

[He goes out into the drawing-room; and **FREDA** stands restlessly tapping her foot against the bottom stair. With a flutter of skirts **CHRISTINE KEITH** comes rapidly down. She is a nice-looking, fresh-coloured young woman in a low-necked dress.

CHRISTINE
Hullo, Freda! How are YOU?

FREDA
Quite well, thank you, Miss Christine—Mrs. Keith, I mean. My lady told me to give you these.

CHRISTINE [Taking the roses]
Oh! Thanks! How sweet of mother!

FREDA [In a quick, toneless voice]
The others are for Miss Lanfarne. My lady thought white would suit her better.

CHRISTINE
They suit you in that black dress.

[**FREDA** lowers the roses quickly.

What do you think of Joan's engagement?

FREDA
It's very nice for her.

CHRISTINE
I say, Freda, have they been going hard at rehearsals?

FREDA
Every day. Miss Dot gets very cross, stage-managing.

CHRISTINE
I do hate learning a part. Thanks awfully for unpacking.
Any news?

FREDA [In the same quick, dull voice]
The under-keeper, Dunning, won't marry Rose Taylor, after all.

CHRISTINE
What a shame! But I say that's serious. I thought there was—she was—I mean—

FREDA
He's taken up with another girl, they say.

CHRISTINE
Too bad!

[Pinning the roses.

D'you know if Mr. Bill's come?

FREDA [With a swift upward look]
Yes, by the six-forty.

[**RONALD KEITH** comes slowly down, a weathered firm-lipped man, in evening dress, with eyelids half drawn over his keen eyes, and the air of a horseman.

KEITH
Hallo! Roses in December. I say, Freda, your father missed a wigging this morning when they drew blank at Warnham's spinney. Where's that litter of little foxes?

FREDA [Smiling faintly]

I expect father knows, Captain Keith.

KEITH
You bet he does. Emigration? Or thin air? What?

CHRISTINE
Studdenham'd never shoot a fox, Ronny. He's been here since the flood.

KEITH
There's more ways of killing a cat—eh, Freda?

CHRISTINE [Moving with her husband towards the drawing-room]
Young Dunning won't marry that girl, Ronny.

KEITH
Phew! Wouldn't be in his shoes, then! Sir William'll never keep a servant who's made a scandal in the village, old girl. Bill come?

[As they disappear from the hall, **JOHN LATTER** in a clergyman's evening dress, comes sedately downstairs, a tall, rather pale young man, with something in him, as it were, both of heaven, and a drawing-room. He passes **FREDA** with a formal little nod. **HAROLD**, a fresh-cheeked, cheery-looking youth, comes down, three steps at a time.

HAROLD
Hallo, Freda! Patience on the monument. Let's have a sniff! For Miss Lanfarne? Bill come down yet?

FREDA
No, Mr. Harold.

[**HAROLD** crosses the hall, whistling, and follows **LATTER** into the drawing-room. There is the sound of a scuffle above, and a voice crying: "Shut up, Dot!" And **JOAN** comes down screwing her head back. She is pretty and small, with large clinging eyes.

JOAN
Am I all right behind, Freda? That beast, Dot!

FREDA
Quite, Miss Joan.

[**DOT'S** face, like a full moon, appears over the upper banisters. She too comes running down, a frank figure, with the face of a rebel.

DOT
You little being!

JOAN [Flying towards the drawing-roam, is overtaken at the door]
Oh! Dot! You're pinching!

[As they disappear into the drawing-room, **MABEL LANFARNE**, a tall girl with a rather charming Irish face, comes slowly down. And at sight of her **FREDA'S** whole figure becomes set and meaningfull.

FREDA
For you, Miss Lanfarne, from my lady.

MABEL [In whose speech is a touch of wilful Irishry]
How sweet!

[Fastening the roses.

And how are you, Freda?

FREDA
Very well, thank you.

MABEL
And your father? Hope he's going to let me come out with the guns again.

FREDA [Stolidly]
He'll be delighted, I'm sure.

MABEL
Ye-es! I haven't forgotten his face-last time.

FREDA
You stood with Mr. Bill. He's better to stand with than Mr. Harold, or Captain Keith?

MABEL
He didn't touch a feather, that day.

FREDA
People don't when they're anxious to do their best.

[A gong sounds. And **MABEL LANFARNE**, giving **FREDA** a rather inquisitive stare, moves on to the drawing-room. Left alone without the roses, **FREDA** still lingers. At the slamming of a door above, and hasty footsteps, she shrinks back against the stairs. **BILL** runs down, and comes on her suddenly. He is a tall, good-looking edition of his father, with the same stubborn look of veiled choler.

BILL
Freda! [And as she shrinks still further back] what's the matter?

[Then at some sound he looks round uneasily and draws away from her.

Aren't you glad to see me?

FREDA
I've something to say to you, Mr. Bill. After dinner.

BILL
Mister—?

[She passes him, and rushes away upstairs. And **BILL**, who stands frowning and looking after her, recovers himself sharply as the drawing-room door is opened, and **SIR WILLIAM** and **MISS LANFARNE** come forth, followed by **KEITH, DOT, HAROLD, CHRISTINE, LATTER**, and **JOAN**, all leaning across each other, and talking. By herself, behind them, comes **LADY CHESHIRE**, a refined-looking woman of fifty, with silvery dark hair, and an expression at once gentle, and ironic. They move across the hall towards the dining-room.

SIR WILLIAM
Ah! Bill.

MABEL
How do you do?

KEITH
How are you, old chap?

DOT [Gloomily]
Do you know your part?

HAROLD
Hallo, old man!

[**CHRISTINE** gives her brother a flying kiss. **JOAN** and **LATTER** pause and look at him shyly without speech.

BILL [Putting his hand on **JOAN'S** shoulder]
Good luck, you two!
Well mother?

LADY CHESHIRE
Well, my dear boy! Nice to see you at last. What a long time!

[She draws his arm through hers, and they move towards the dining-room.

The curtain falls.

The curtain rises again at once.

SCENE II

CHRISTINE, LADY CHESHIRE, DOT, MABEL LANFARNE, and **JOAN**, are returning to the hall after dinner.

CHRISTINE [in a low voice]
Mother, is it true about young Dunning and Rose Taylor?

LADY CHESHIRE
I'm afraid so, dear.

CHRISTINE
But can't they be—

DOT
Ah! ah-h!

[**CHRISTINE** and her mother are silent.

My child, I'm not the young person.

CHRISTINE
No, of course not—only—

[Nodding towards **JOAN** and **MABEL**.

DOT
Look here! This is just an instance of what I hate.

LADY CHESHIRE
My dear? Another one?

DOT
Yes, mother, and don't you pretend you don't understand, because you know you do.

CHRISTINE
Instance? Of what?

[**JOAN** and **MABEL** have ceased talking, and listen, still at the fire.

DOT
Humbug, of course. Why should you want them to marry, if he's tired of her?

CHRISTINE [Ironically]
Well! If your imagination doesn't carry you as far as that!

DOT
When people marry, do you believe they ought to be in love with each other?

CHRISTINE [With a shrug]
That's not the point.

DOT

Oh? Were you in love with Ronny?

CHRISTINE
Don't be idiotic!

DOT
Would you have married him if you hadn't been?

CHRISTINE
Of course not!

JOAN
Dot! You are!—

DOT
Hallo! my little snipe!

LADY CHESHIRE
Dot, dear!

DOT
Don't shut me up, mother! [To **JOAN**.] Are you in love with John?

[**JOAN** turns hurriedly to the fire.

Would you be going to marry him if you were not?

CHRISTINE
You are a brute, Dot.

DOT
Is Mabel in love with—whoever she is in love with?

MABEL
And I wonder who that is.

DOT
Well, would you marry him if you weren't?

MABEL
No, I would not.

DOT
Now, mother; did you love father?

CHRISTINE
Dot, you really are awful.

DOT [Rueful and detached]
Well, it is a bit too thick, perhaps.

JOAN
Dot!

DOT
Well, mother, did you—I mean quite calmly?

LADY CHESHIRE
Yes, dear, quite calmly.

DOT
Would you have married him if you hadn't?

[**LADY CHESHIRE** shakes her head]

Then we're all agreed!

MABEL
Except yourself.

DOT [Grimly]
Even if I loved him, he might think himself lucky if I married him.

MABEL
Indeed, and I'm not so sure.

DOT [Making a face at her]
What I was going to—

LADY CHESHIRE
But don't you think, dear, you'd better not?

DOT
Well, I won't say what I was going to say, but what I do say is—Why the devil—

LADY CHESHIRE
Quite so, Dot!

DOT [A little disconcerted]
If they're tired of each other, they ought not to marry, and if father's going to make them—

CHRISTINE
You don't understand in the least. It's for the sake of the—

DOT
Out with it, Old Sweetness! The approaching infant! God bless it!

[There is a sudden silence, for **KEITH** and **LATTER** are seen coming from the dining-room.

LATTER
That must be so, Ronny.

KEITH
No, John; not a bit of it!

LATTER
You don't think!

KEITH
Good Gad, who wants to think after dinner!

DOT
Come on! Let's play pool.

[She turns at the billiard-room door.

Look here! Rehearsal to-morrow is directly after breakfast; from "Eccles enters breathless" to the end.

MABEL
Whatever made you choose "Caste," Dot? You know it's awfully difficult.

DOT
Because it's the only play that's not too advanced.

[The **GIRLS** all go into the billiard-room.

LADY CHESHIRE
Where's Bill, Ronny?

KEITH [With a grimace]
I rather think Sir William and he are in Committee of Supply—Mem-Sahib.

LADY CHESHIRE
Oh!

She looks uneasily at the dining-room; then follows the girls out.

LATTER [In the tone of one resuming an argument]
There can't be two opinions about it, Ronny. Young Dunning's refusal is simply indefensible.

KEITH
I don't agree a bit, John.

LATTER

Of course, if you won't listen.

KEITH [Clipping a cigar]
Draw it mild, my dear chap. We've had the whole thing over twice at least.

LATTER
My point is this—

KEITH [Regarding **LATTER** quizzically with his half-closed eyes]
I know—I know—but the point is, how far your point is simply professional.

LATTER
If a man wrongs a woman, he ought to right her again. There's no answer to that.

KEITH
It all depends.

LATTER
That's rank opportunism.

KEITH
Rats! Look here—Oh! hang it, John, one can't argue this out with a parson.

LATTER [Frigidly]
Why not?

HAROLD [Who has entered from the dining-room]
Pull devil, pull baker!

KEITH
Shut up, Harold!

LATTER
"To play the game" is the religion even of the Army.

KEITH
Exactly, but what is the game?

LATTER
What else can it be in this case?

KEITH
You're too puritanical, young John. You can't help it—line of country laid down for you. All drag-huntin'! What!

LATTER [With concentration]
Look here!

HAROLD [Imitating the action of a man pulling at a horse's head]
'Come hup, I say, you hugly beast!'

KEITH [To **LATTER**]
You're not going to draw me, old chap. You don't see where you'd land us all.

[He smokes calmly.

LATTER
How do you imagine vice takes its rise? From precisely this sort of thing of young Dunning's.

KEITH
From human nature, I should have thought, John. I admit that I don't like a fellow's leavin' a girl in the lurch; but I don't see the use in drawin' hard and fast rules. You only have to break 'em. Sir William and you would just tie Dunning and the girl up together, willy-nilly, to save appearances, and ten to one but there'll be the deuce to pay in a year's time. You can take a horse to the water, you can't make him drink.

LATTER
I entirely and absolutely disagree with you.

HAROLD
Good old John!

LATTER
At all events we know where your principles take you.

KEITH [Rather dangerously]
Where, please?

[**HAROLD** turns up his eyes, and points downwards.

Dry up, Harold!

LATTER
Did you ever hear the story of Faust?

KEITH
Now look here, John; with all due respect to your cloth, and all the politeness in the world, you may go to-blazes.

LATTER
Well, I must say, Ronny—of all the rude boors—

[He turns towards the billiard-room.

KEITH
Sorry I smashed the glass, old chap.

[**LATTER** passes out. There comes a mingled sound through the opened door, of female voices, laughter, and the click of billiard balls, dipped of by the sudden closing of the door.

KEITH [Impersonally]
Deuced odd, the way a parson puts one's back up! Because you know I agree with him really; young Dunning ought to play the game; and I hope Sir William'll make him.

[The butler **JACKSON** has entered from the door under the stairs followed by the keeper **STUDDENHAM**, a man between fifty and sixty, in a full-skirted coat with big pockets, cord breeches, and gaiters; he has a steady self respecting weathered face, with blue eyes and a short grey beard, which has obviously once been red.

KEITH
Hullo! Studdenham!

STUDDENHAM [Touching his forehead]
Evenin', Captain Keith.

JACKSON
Sir William still in the dining-room with Mr. Bill, sir?

HAROLD [With a grimace]
He is, Jackson.

[**JACKSON** goes out to the dining-room.

KEITH
You've shot no pheasants yet, Studdenham?

STUDDENHAM
No, Sir. Only birds. We'll be doin' the spinneys and the home covert while you're down.

KEITH
I say, talkin' of spinneys—

[He breaks off sharply, and goes out with **HAROLD** into the billiard-room. **SIR WILLIAM** enters from the dining-room, applying a gold toothpick to his front teeth.

SIR WILLIAM
Ah! Studdenham. Bad business this, about young Dunning!

STUDDENHAM
Yes, Sir William.

SIR WILLIAM
He definitely refuses to marry her?

STUDDENHAM

He does that.

SIR WILLIAM

That won't do, you know. What reason does he give?

STUDDENHAM

Won't say other than that he don't want no more to do with her.

SIR WILLIAM

God bless me! That's not a reason. I can't have a keeper of mine playing fast and loose in the village like this.

[Turning to **LADY CHESHIRE**, who has come in from the billiard-room.

That affair of young Dunning's, my dear.

LADY CHESHIRE

Oh! Yes! I'm so sorry, Studdenham. The poor girl!

STUDDENHAM [Respectfully]

Fancy he's got a feeling she's not his equal, now, my lady.

LATTER [To herself]

Yes, I suppose he has made her his superior.

SIR WILLIAM

What? Eh! Quite! Quite! I was just telling Studdenham the fellow must set the matter straight. We can't have open scandals in the village. If he wants to keep his place he must marry her at once.

LADY CHESHIRE [To her **HUSBAND** in a low voice]

Is it right to force them? Do you know what the girl wishes, Studdenham?

STUDDENHAM

Shows a spirit, my lady—says she'll have him—willin' or not.

LADY CHESHIRE

A spirit? I see. If they marry like that they're sure to be miserable.

SIR WILLIAM

What! Doesn't follow at all. Besides, my dear, you ought to know by this time, there's an unwritten law in these matters. They're perfectly well aware that when there are consequences, they have to take them.

STUDDENHAM

Some o' these young people, my lady, they don't put two and two together no more than an old cock pheasant.

SIR WILLIAM
I'll give him till to-morrow. If he remains obstinate, he'll have to go; he'll get no character, Studdenham. Let him know what I've said. I like the fellow, he's a good keeper. I don't want to lose him. But this sort of thing I won't have. He must toe the mark or take himself off. Is he up here to-night?

STUDDENHAM
Hangin' partridges, Sir William. Will you have him in?

SIR WILLIAM [Hesitating]
Yes—yes. I'll see him.

STUDDENHAM
Good-night to you, my lady.

LADY CHESHIRE
Freda's not looking well, Studdenham.

STUDDENHAM
She's a bit pernickitty with her food, that's where it is.

LADY CHESHIRE
I must try and make her eat.

SIR WILLIAM
Oh! Studdenham. We'll shoot the home covert first. What did we get last year?

STUDDENHAM [Producing the game-book; but without reference to it]
Two hundred and fifty-three pheasants, eleven hares, fifty-two rabbits, three woodcock, sundry.

SIR WILLIAM
Sundry? Didn't include a fox did it? [Gravely] I was seriously upset this morning at Warnham's spinney—

SUDDENHAM [Very gravely]
You don't say, Sir William; that four-year-old he du look a handful!

SIR WILLIAM [With a sharp look]
You know well enough what I mean.

STUDDENHAM [Unmoved]
Shall I send young Dunning, Sir William?

[**SIR WILLIAM** gives a short, sharp nod, and **STUDDENHAM** retires by the door under the stairs.

SIR WILLIAM
Old fox!

LADY CHESHIRE

Don't be too hard on Dunning. He's very young.

SIR WILLIAM [Patting her arm]
My dear, you don't understand young fellows, how should you?

LADY CHESHIRE [With her faint irony]
A husband and two sons not counting.

[Then as the door under the stairs is opened.

Bill, now do—

SIR WILLIAM
I'll be gentle with him. [Sharply] Come in!

[**LADY CHESHIRE** retires to the billiard-room. She gives a look back and a half smile at young **DUNNING**, a fair young man dressed in broom cords and leggings, and holding his cap in his hand; then goes out.

SIR WILLIAM
Evenin', Dunning.

DUNNING [Twisting his cap]
Evenin', Sir William.

SIR WILLIAM
Studdenham's told you what I want to see you about?

DUNNING
Yes, Sir.

SIR WILLIAM
The thing's in your hands. Take it or leave it. I don't put pressure on you. I simply won't have this sort of thing on my estate.

DUNNING
I'd like to say, Sir William, that she—

[He stops.

SIR WILLIAM
Yes, I daresay-Six of one and half a dozen of the other. Can't go into that.

DUNNING
No, Sir William.

SIR WILLIAM
I'm quite mild with you. This is your first place. If you leave here you'll get no character.

DUNNING
I never meant any harm, sir.

SIR WILLIAM
My good fellow, you know the custom of the country.

DUNNING
Yes, Sir William, but—

SIR WILLIAM
You should have looked before you leaped. I'm not forcing you. If you refuse you must go, that's all.

DUNNING
Yes. Sir William.

SIR WILLIAM
Well, now go along and take a day to think it over.

[**BILL**, who has sauntered moody from the dining room, stands by the stairs listening. Catching sight of him, **DUNNING** raises his hand to his forelock.

DUNNING
Very good, Sir William.

[He turns, fumbles, and turns again.

My old mother's dependent on me—

SIR WILLIAM
Now, Dunning, I've no more to say.

[**DUNNING** goes sadly away under the stairs.

SIR WILLIAM [Following]
And look here! Just understand this

[He too goes out....

[**BILL**, lighting a cigarette, has approached the writing-table. He looks very glum. The billiard-room door is flung open. **MABEL LANFARNE** appears, and makes him a little curtsey.

MABEL
Against my will I am bidden to bring you in to pool.

BILL
Sorry! I've got letters.

MABEL

You seem to have become very conscientious.

BILL
Oh! I don't know.

MABEL
Do you remember the last day of the covert shooting?

BILL
I do.

MABEL [Suddenly]
What a pretty girl Freda Studdenham's grown!

BILL
Has she?

MABEL
"She walks in beauty."

BILL
Really? Hadn't noticed.

MABEL
Have you been taking lessons in conversation?

BILL
Don't think so.

MABEL
Oh!

[There is a silence.

Mr. Cheshire!

BILL
Miss Lanfarne!

MABEL
What's the matter with you? Aren't you rather queer, considering that I don't bite, and was rather a pal!

BILL [Stolidly]
I'm sorry.

[Then seeing that his mother has come in from the billiard-room, he sits down at the writing-table.

LADY CHESHIRE

Mabel, dear, do take my cue. Won't you play too, Bill, and try and stop Ronny, he's too terrible?

BILL
Thanks. I've got these letters.

[**MABEL** taking the cue passes back into the billiard-room, whence comes out the sound of talk and laughter.

LADY CHESHIRE [Going over and standing behind her son's chair]
Anything wrong, darling?

BILL
Nothing, thanks. [Suddenly] I say, I wish you hadn't asked that girl here.

LADY CHESHIRE
Mabel! Why? She's wanted for rehearsals. I thought you got on so well with her last Christmas.

BILL [With a sort of sullen exasperation.]
A year ago.

LADY CHESHIRE
The girls like her, so does your father; personally I must say I think she's rather nice and Irish.

BILL
She's all right, I daresay.

[He looks round as if to show his mother that he wishes to be left alone. But **LADY CHESHIRE**, having seen that he is about to look at her, is not looking at him.

LADY CHESHIRE
I'm afraid your father's been talking to you, Bill.

BILL
He has.

LADY CHESHIRE
Debts? Do try and make allowances.

[With a faint smile.

Of course he is a little—

BILL
He is.

LADY CHESHIRE
I wish I could—

BILL
Oh, Lord! Don't you get mixed up in it!

LADY CHESHIRE
It seems almost a pity that you told him.

BILL
He wrote and asked me point blank what I owed.

LADY CHESHIRE
Oh!

[Forcing herself to speak in a casual voice.

I happen to have a little money, Bill—I think it would be simpler if—

BILL
Now look here, mother, you've tried that before. I can't help spending money, I never shall be able, unless I go to the Colonies, or something of the kind.

LADY CHESHIRE
Don't talk like that, dear!

BILL
I would, for two straws!

LADY CHESHIRE
It's only because your father thinks such a lot of the place, and the name, and your career. The Cheshires are all like that. They've been here so long; they're all—root.

BILL
Deuced funny business my career will be, I expect!

LADY CHESHIRE [Fluttering, but restraining herself lest he should see]
But, Bill, why must you spend more than your allowance?

BILL
Why—anything? I didn't make myself.

LADY CHESHIRE
I'm afraid we did that. It was inconsiderate, perhaps.

BILL
Yes, you'd better have left me out.

LADY CHESHIRE
But why are you so—Only a little fuss about money!

BILL
Ye-es.

LADY CHESHIRE
You're not keeping anything from me, are you?

BILL [Facing her]
No.

[He then turns very deliberately to the writing things, and takes up a pen.

I must write these letters, please.

LADY CHESHIRE
Bill, if there's any real trouble, you will tell me, won't you?

BILL
There's nothing whatever.

[He suddenly gets up and walks about. **LADY CHESHIRE**, too, moves over to the fireplace, and after an uneasy look at him, turns to the fire. Then, as if trying to switch of his mood, she changes the subject abruptly.

LADY CHESHIRE
Isn't it a pity about young Dunning? I'm so sorry for Rose Taylor.

[There is a silence. Stealthily under the staircase **FREDA** has entered, and seeing only **BILL**, advances to speak to him.

BILL [Suddenly]
Oh! well,—you can't help these things in the country.

As he speaks, **FREDA** stops dead, perceiving that he is not alone; BILL, too, catching sight of her, starts.

LADY CHESHIRE [Still speaking to the fire]
It seems dreadful to force him. I do so believe in people doing things of their own accord.

[Then seeing **FREDA** standing so uncertainly by the stairs.

Do you want me, Freda?

FREDA
Only your cloak, my lady. Shall I—begin it?

[At this moment **SIR WILLIAM** enters from the drawing-room.

LADY CHESHIRE
Yes, yes.

SIR WILLIAM [Genially]
Can you give me another five minutes, Bill?

[Pointing to the billiard-room.

We'll come directly, my dear.

[**FREDA**, with a look at **BILL**, has gone back whence she came; and **LADY CHESHIRE** goes reluctantly away into the billiard-room.

SIR WILLIAM
I shall give young Dunning short shrift.

[He moves over to the fireplace and divides hip coat-tails.

Now, about you, Bill! I don't want to bully you the moment you come down, but you know, this can't go on. I've paid your debts twice. Shan't pay them this time unless I see a disposition to change your mode of life.

[A pause.

You get your extravagance from your mother. She's very queer—

[A pause.

—All the Winterleighs are like that about money....

BILL
Mother's particularly generous, if that's what you mean.

SIR WILLIAM [Drily]
We will put it that way.

[A pause.

At the present moment you owe, as I understand it, eleven hundred pounds.

BILL
About that.

SIR WILLIAM
Mere flea-bite.

[A pause]

I've a proposition to make.

BILL
Won't it do to-morrow, sir?

SIR WILLIAM
"To-morrow" appears to be your motto in life.

BILL
Thanks!

SIR WILLIAM
I'm anxious to change it to-day.

[**BILL** looks at him in silence.

It's time you took your position seriously, instead of hanging about town, racing, and playing polo, and what not.

BILL
Go ahead!

[At something dangerous in his voice, **SIR WILLIAM** modifies his attitude.

SIR,WILLIAM
The proposition's very simple. I can't suppose anything so rational and to your advantage will appeal to you, but [drily] I mention it. Marry a nice girl, settle down, and stand for the division; you can have the Dower House and fifteen hundred a year, and I'll pay your debts into the bargain. If you're elected I'll make it two thousand. Plenty of time to work up the constituency before we kick out these infernal Rads. Carpetbagger against you; if you go hard at it in the summer, it'll be odd if you don't manage to get in your three days a week, next season. You can take Rocketer and that four-year-old—he's well up to your weight, fully eight and a half inches of bone. You'll only want one other. And if Miss—if your wife means to hunt—

BILL
You've chosen my wife, then?

SIR WILLIAM [With a quick look]
I imagine, you've some girl in your mind.

BILL
Ah!

SIR WILLIAM
Used not to be unnatural at your age. I married your mother at twenty-eight. Here you are, eldest son of a family that stands for something. The more I see of the times the more I'm convinced that everybody who is anybody has got to buckle to, and save the landmarks left. Unless we're true to our caste, and prepared to work for it, the landed classes are going to go under to this infernal democratic spirit in the air. The outlook's very serious. We're threatened in a hundred ways. If you mean business, you'll want a wife. When I came into the property I should have been lost without your mother.

BILL
I thought this was coming.

SIR WILLIAM [With a certain geniality]
My dear fellow, I don't want to put a pistol to your head. You've had a slack rein so far. I've never objected to your sowing a few wild oats-so long as you —er—

[Unseen by **SIR WILLIAM, BILL** makes a sudden movement.

Short of that—at all events, I've not inquired into your affairs. I can only judge by the—er—pecuniary evidence you've been good enough to afford me from time to time. I imagine you've lived like a good many young men in your position—I'm not blaming you, but there's a time for all things.

BILL
Why don't you say outright that you want me to marry Mabel Lanfarne?

SIR WILLIAM
Well, I do. Girl's a nice one. Good family—got a little money—rides well. Isn't she good-looking enough for you, or what?

BILL
Quite, thanks.

SIR WILLIAM
I understood from your mother that you and she were on good terms.

BILL
Please don't drag mother into it.

SIR WILLIAM [With dangerous politeness]
Perhaps you'll be good enough to state your objections.

BILL
Must we go on with this?

SIR WILLIAM
I've never asked you to do anything for me before; I expect you to pay attention now. I've no wish to dragoon you into this particular marriage. If you don't care for Miss Lanfarne, marry a girl you're fond of.

BILL
I refuse.

SIR WILLIAM
In that case you know what to look out for.

[With a sudden rush of choler.

You young....

[He checks himself and stands glaring at **BILL**, who glares back at him.

This means, I suppose, that you've got some entanglement or other.

BILL
Suppose what you like, sir.

SIR WILLIAM
I warn you, if you play the blackguard—

BILL
You can't force me like young Dunning.

[Hearing the raised voices **LADY CHESHIRE** has come back from the billiard-room.

LADY CHESHIRE [Closing the door]
What is it?

SIR WILLIAM
You deliberately refuse! Go away, Dorothy.

LADY CHESHIRE [Resolutely]
I haven't seen Bill for two months.

SIR WILLIAM
What! [Hesitating] Well—we must talk it over again.

LADY CHESHIRE
Come to the billiard-room, both of you! Bill, do finish those letters!

[With a deft movement she draws **SIR WILLIAM** toward the billiard-room, and glances back at **BILL** before going out, but he has turned to the writing-table. When the door is closed, **BILL** looks into the drawing-room, them opens the door under the stairs; and backing away towards the writing-table, sits down there, and takes up a pen. **FREDA** who has evidently been waiting, comes in and stands by the table.

BILL
I say, this is dangerous, you know.

FREDA
Yes—but I must.

BILL
Well, then—[With natural recklessness] Aren't you going to kiss me?

[Without moving she looks at him with a sort of miserable inquiry.

BILL
Do you know you haven't seen me for eight weeks?

FREDA
Quite—long enough—for you to have forgotten.

BILL
Forgotten! I don't forget people so soon.

FREDA
No?

BILL
What's the matter with you, Freda?

FREDA [After a long look]
It'll never be as it was.

BILL [Jumping up]
How d'you mean?

FREDA
I've got something for you.

[She takes a diamond ring out of her dress and holds it out to him]

I've not worn it since Cromer.

BILL
Now, look here

FREDA
I've had my holiday; I shan't get another in a hurry.

BILL
Freda!

FREDA
You'll be glad to be free. That fortnight's all you really loved me in.

BILL [Putting his hands on her arms]
I swear—

FREDA [Between her teeth]
Miss Lanfarne need never know about me.

BILL
So that's it! I've told you a dozen times—nothing's changed.

[**FREDA** looks at him and smiles.

BILL
Oh! very well! If you will make yourself miserable.

FREDA
Everybody will be pleased.

BILL
At what?

FREDA
When you marry her.

BILL
This is too bad.

FREDA
It's what always happens—even when it's not a—gentleman.

BILL
That's enough.

FREDA
But I'm not like that girl down in the village. You needn't be afraid I'll say anything when—it comes. That's what I had to tell you.

BILL
What!

FREDA
I can keep a secret.

BILL
Do you mean this?

[She bows her head.

BILL
Good God!

FREDA
Father brought me up not to whine. Like the puppies when they hold them up by their tails.

[With a sudden break in her voice.

Oh! Bill!

BILL [With his head down, seizing her hands]
Freda!

[He breaks away from her towards the fire.

Good God!

[She stands looking at him, then quietly slips away by the door under the staircase. **BILL** turns to speak to her, and sees that she has gone. He walks up to the fireplace, and grips the mantelpiece.

BILL
By Jove! This is—!

The curtain falls.

The scene is Lady Cheshire's morning room, at ten o'clock on the following day. It is a pretty room, with white panelled walls; and chrysanthemums and carmine lilies in bowls. A large bow window overlooks the park under a sou'-westerly sky. A piano stands open; a fire is burning; and the morning's correspondence is scattered on a writing-table. Doors opposite each other lead to the maid's workroom, and to a corridor. **LADY CHESHIRE** is standing in the middle of the room, looking at an opera cloak, which **FREDA** is holding out.

LADY CHESHIRE
Well, Freda, suppose you just give it up!

FREDA
I don't like to be beaten.

LADY CHESHIRE
You're not to worry over your work. And by the way, I promised your father to make you eat more.

[**FREDA** smiles.

LADY CHESHIRE
It's all very well to smile. You want bracing up. Now don't be naughty. I shall give you a tonic. And I think you had better put that cloak away.

FREDA
I'd rather have one more try, my lady.

LADY CHESHIRE [Sitting doom at her writing-table]
Very well.

[**FREDA** goes out into her workroom, as **JACKSON** comes in from the corridor.

JACKSON
Excuse me, my lady. There's a young woman from the village, says you wanted to see her.

LADY CHESHIRE
Rose Taylor? Ask her to come in. Oh! and Jackson the car for the meet please at half-past ten.

[**JACKSON** having bowed and withdrawn, **LADY CHESHIRE** rises with worked signs of nervousness, which she has only just suppressed, when **ROSE TAYLOR**, a stolid country girl, comes in and stands waiting by the door.

LADY CHESHIRE
Well, Rose. Do come in!

[**ROSE** advances perhaps a couple of steps.

LADY CHESHIRE
I just wondered whether you'd like to ask my advice. Your engagement with Dunning's broken off, isn't it?

ROSE
Yes—but I've told him he's got to marry me.

LADY CHESHIRE
I see! And you think that'll be the wisest thing?

ROSE [Stolidly]
I don't know, my lady. He's got to.

LADY CHESHIRE
I do hope you're a little fond of him still.

ROSE
I'm not. He don't deserve it.

LADY CHESHIRE
And—do you think he's quite lost his affection for you?

ROSE
I suppose so, else he wouldn't treat me as he's done. He's after that—that—He didn't ought to treat me as if I was dead.

LADY CHESHIRE
No, no—of course. But you will think it all well over, won't you?

ROSE

I've a—got nothing to think over, except what I know of.

LADY CHESHIRE

But for you both to marry in that spirit! You know it's for life, Rose.

[Looking into her face.

I'm always ready to help you.

ROSE [Dropping a very slight curtsey]

Thank you, my lady, but I think he ought to marry me. I've told him he ought.

LADY CHESHIRE [Sighing]

Well, that's all I wanted to say. It's a question of your self-respect; I can't give you any real advice. But just remember that if you want a friend—

ROSE [With a gulp]

I'm not so 'ard, really. I only want him to do what's right by me.

LADY CHESHIRE [With a little lift of her eyebrow—gently]

Yes, yes—I see.

ROSE [Glancing back at the door]

I don't like meeting the servants.

LADY CHESHIRE

Come along, I'll take you out another way.

[As they reach the door, **DOT** comes in.

DOT [With a glance at **ROSE**]

Can we have this room for the mouldy rehearsal, Mother?

LADY CHESHIRE

Yes, dear, you can air it here.

[Holding the door open for **ROSE** she follows her out. And **DOT**, with a book of "Caste" in her hand, arranges the room according to a diagram.

DOT

Chair—chair—table—chair—Dash! Table—piano—fire—window!

[Producing a pocket comb.

Comb for Eccles. Cradle?—Cradle—

[She viciously dumps a waste-paper basket down, and drops a footstool into it]

Brat!

[Then reading from the book gloomily.

"Enter Eccles breathless. Esther and Polly rise-Esther puts on lid of bandbox." Bandbox!

[Searching for something to represent a bandbox, she opens the workroom door.

DOT
Freda?

[**FREDA** comes in.

DOT
I say, Freda. Anything the matter? You seem awfully down.

[**FREDA** does not answer.

DOT
You haven't looked anything of a lollipop lately.

FREDA
I'm quite all right, thank you, Miss Dot.

DOT
Has Mother been givin' you a tonic?

FREDA [Smiling a little]
Not yet.

DOT
That doesn't account for it then.

[With a sudden warm impulse]

What is it, Freda?

FREDA
Nothing.

DOT [Switching of on a different line of thought]
Are you very busy this morning?

FREDA
Only this cloak for my lady.

DOT

Oh! that can wait. I may have to get you in to prompt, if I can't keep 'em straight. [Gloomily] They stray so. Would you mind?

FREDA [Stolidly]
I shall be very glad, Miss Dot.

DOT [Eyeing her dubiously]
All right. Let's see—what did I want?

[**JOAN** has come in.

JOAN
Look here, Dot; about the baby in this scene. I'm sure I ought to make more of it.

DOT
Romantic little beast!

[She plucks the footstool out by one ear, and holds it forth.

Let's see you try!

JOAN [Recoiling]
But, Dot, what are we really going to have for the baby? I can't rehearse with that thing. Can't you suggest something, Freda?

FREDA
Borrow a real one, Miss Joan. There are some that don't count much.

JOAN
Freda, how horrible!

DOT [Dropping the footstool back into the basket]
You'll just put up with what you're given.

[Then as **CHRISTINE** and **MABEL LANFARNE** come in, **FREDA** turns abruptly and goes out.

DOT
Buck up! Where are Bill and Harold? [To **JOAN**] Go and find them, mouse-cat.

[But **BILL** and **HAROLD**, followed by **LATTER**, are already in the doorway. They come in, and **LATTER**, stumbling over the waste-paper basket, takes it up to improve its position.

DOT
Drop that cradle, John!

[As he picks the footstool out of it.

Leave the baby in! Now then! Bill, you enter there!

[She points to the workroom door where **BILL** and **MABEL** range themselves close to the piano; while **HAROLD** goes to the window.

John! get off the stage! Now then, "Eccles enters breathless, Esther and Polly rise." Wait a minute. I know now.

[She opens the workroom door.

Freda, I wanted a bandbox.

HAROLD [Cheerfully]
I hate beginning to rehearse, you know, you feel such a fool.

DOT [With her bandbox-gloomily]
You'll feel more of a fool when you have begun. [To **BILL**, who is staring into the workroom] Shut the door. Now.

[**BILL** shuts the door.

LATTER [Advancing]
Look here! I want to clear up a point of psychology before we start.

DOT
Good Lord!

LATTER
When I bring in the milk—ought I to bring it in seriously—as if I were accustomed—I mean, I maintain that if I'm—

JOAN
Oh! John, but I don't think it's meant that you should—

DOT
Shut up! Go back, John! Blow the milk! Begin, begin, begin! Bill!

LATTER [Turning round and again advancing]
But I think you underrate the importance of my entrance altogether.

MABEL
Oh! no, Mr. Latter!

LATTER
I don't in the least want to destroy the balance of the scene, but I do want to be clear about the spirit. What is the spirit?

DOT [With gloom]

Rollicking!

LATTER
Well, I don't think so. We shall run a great risk, with this play, if we rollick.

DOT
Shall we? Now look here—!

MABEL [Softly to **BILL**]
Mr. Cheshire!

BILL [Desperately]
Let's get on!

DOT [Waving **LATTER** back]
Begin, begin! At last!

[But **JACKSON** has came in.

JACKSON [To **CHRISTINE**]
Studdenham says, Mm, if the young ladies want to see the spaniel pups, he's brought 'em round.

JOAN [Starting up]
Oh! come 'on, John!

[She flies towards the door, followed by **LATTER**.

DOT [Gesticulating with her book]
Stop! You—

[**CHRISTINE** and **HAROLD** also rush past.

DOT [Despairingly]
First pick!

[Tearing her hair.

Pigs! Devils!

[She rushes after them. **BILL** and **MABEL** are left alone.

MABEL [Mockingly]
And don't you want one of the spaniel pups?

BILL [Painfully reserved and sullen, and conscious of the workroom door]
Can't keep a dog in town. You can have one, if you like. The breeding's all right.

MABEL

Sixth Pick?

BILL
The girls'll give you one of theirs. They only fancy they want 'em.

MABEL [Moving nearer to him, with her hands clasped behind her]
You know, you remind me awfully of your father. Except that you're not nearly so polite. I don't understand you English-lords of the soil. The way you have of disposing of your females. [With a sudden change of voice] What was the matter with you last night? [Softly] Won't you tell me?

BILL
Nothing to tell.

MABEL
Ah! no, Mr. Bill.

BILL [Almost succumbing to her voice—then sullenly]
Worried, I suppose.

MABEL [Returning to her mocking]
Quite got over it?

BILL
Don't chaff me, please.

MABEL
You really are rather formidable.

BILL
Thanks.

MABEL
But, you know, I love to cross a field where there's a bull.

BILL
Really! Very interesting.

MABEL
The way of their only seeing one thing at a time.

[She moves back as he advances.

And overturning people on the journey.

BILL
Hadn't you better be a little careful?

MABEL

And never to see the hedge until they're stuck in it. And then straight from that hedge into the opposite one.

BILL [Savagely]
What makes you bait me this morning of all mornings?

MABEL
The beautiful morning! [Suddenly] It must be dull for poor Freda working in there with all this fun going on?

BILL [Glancing at the door]
Fun you call it?

MABEL
To go back to you,—now—Mr. Cheshire.

BILL
No.

MABEL
You always make me feel so Irish. Is it because you're so English, d'you think? Ah! I can see him moving his ears. Now he's pawing the ground—He's started!

BILL
Miss Lanfarne!

MABEL [Still backing away from him, and drawing him on with her eyes and smile]

You can't help coming after me!

[Then with a sudden change to a sort of sierra gravity.

Can you? You'll feel that when I've gone.

[They stand quite still, looking into each other's eyes and **FREDA**, who has opened the door of the workroom stares at them.

MABEL [Seeing her]
Here's the stile. Adieu, Monsieur le taureau!

[She puts her hand behind her, opens the door, and slips through, leaving **BILL** to turn, following the direction of her eyes, and see **FREDA** with the cloak still in her hand.

BILL [Slowly walking towards her]
I haven't slept all night.

FREDA
No?

BILL
Have you been thinking it over?

[**FREDA** gives a bitter little laugh.

BILL
Don't! We must make a plan. I'll get you away. I won't let you suffer. I swear I won't.

FREDA
That will be clever.

BILL
I wish to Heaven my affairs weren't in such a mess.

FREDA
I shall be—all—right, thank you.

BILL
You must think me a blackguard.

[She shakes her head.

Abuse me—say something! Don't look like that!

FREDA
Were you ever really fond of me?

BILL
Of course I was, I am now. Give me your hands.

[She looks at him, then drags her hands from his, and covers her face.

BILL [Clenching his fists]
Look here! I'll prove it.

[Then as she suddenly flings her arms round his neck and clings to him.

There, there!

[There is a click of a door handle. They start away from each other, and see **LADY CHESHIRE** regarding them.

LADY CHESHIRE [Without irony]
I beg your pardon.

[She makes as if to withdraw from an unwarranted intrusion, but suddenly turning, stands, with lips pressed together, waiting.

LADY CHESHIRE
Yes?

[**FREDA** has muffled her face. But **BILL** turns and confronts his mother.

BILL
Don't say anything against her!

LADY CHESHIRE [Tries to speak to him and fails—then to **FREDA**]
Please-go!

BILL [Taking **FREDA'S** arm]
No.

[**LADY CHESHIRE**, after a moment's hesitation, herself moves towards the door.

BILL
Stop, mother!

LADY CHESHIRE
I think perhaps not.

BILL [Looking at **FREDA**, who is cowering as though from a blow]
It's a d—d shame!

LADY CHESHIRE
It is.

BILL [With sudden resolution]
It's not as you think. I'm engaged to be married to her.

[**FREDA** gives him a wild stare, and turns away.

LADY CHESHIRE [Looking from one to the other]
I don't think I—quite—understand.

BILL [With the brutality of his mortification]
What I said was plain enough.

LADY CHESHIRE
Bill!

BILL
I tell you I am going to marry her.

LADY CHESHIRE [To **FREDA**]
Is that true?

[**FREDA** gulps and remains silent.]

BILL
If you want to say anything, say it to me, mother.

LADY CHESHIRE [Gripping the edge of a little table]
Give me a chair, please.

[**BILL** gives her a chair.

LADY CHESHIRE [To **FREDA**]
Please sit down too.

[**FREDA** sits on the piano stool, still turning her face away.

LADY CHESHIRE [Fixing her eyes on **FREDA**]
Now!

BILL
I fell in love with her. And she with me.

LADY CHESHIRE
When?

BILL
In the summer.

LADY CHESHIRE
Ah!

BILL
It wasn't her fault.

LADY CHESHIRE
No?

BILL [With a sort of menace]
Mother!

LADY CHESHIRE
Forgive me, I am not quite used to the idea. You say that you—are engaged?

BILL
Yes.

LADY CHESHIRE
The reasons against such an engagement have occurred to you, I suppose?

[With a sudden change of tone.

Bill! what does it mean?

BILL
If you think she's trapped me into this—

LADY CHESHIRE
I do not. Neither do I think she has been trapped. I think nothing. I understand nothing.

BILL [Grimly]
Good!

LADY CHESHIRE
How long has this-engagement lasted?

BILL [After a silence]
Two months.

LADY CHESHIRE [Suddenly]
This is-this is quite impossible.

BILL
You'll find it isn't.

LADY CHESHIRE
It's simple misery.

BILL [Pointing to the workroom]
Go and wait in there, Freda.

LADY CHESHIRE [Quickly]
And are you still in love with her?

[**FREDA**, moving towards the workroom, smothers a sob.

BILL
Of course I am.

[**FREDA** has gone, and as she goes, **LADY CHESHIRE** rises suddenly, forced by the intense feeling she has been keeping in hand.

LADY CHESHIRE
Bill! Oh, Bill! What does it all mean?

[**BILL**, looking from side to aide, only shrugs his shoulders.

You are not in love with her now. It's no good telling me you are.

BILL
I am.

LADY CHESHIRE
That's not exactly how you would speak if you were.

BILL
She's in love with me.

LADY CHESHIRE [Bitterly]
I suppose so.

BILL
I mean to see that nobody runs her down.

LADY CHESHIRE [With difficulty]
Bill! Am I a hard, or mean woman?

BILL
Mother!

LADY CHESHIRE
It's all your life—and—your father's—and—all of us. I want to understand—I must understand. Have you realised what an awful thins this would be for us all? It's quite impossible that it should go on.

BILL
I'm always in hot water with the Governor, as it is. She and I'll take good care not to be in the way.

LADY CHESHIRE
Tell me everything!

BILL
I have.

LADY CHESHIRE
I'm your mother, Bill.

BILL
What's the good of these questions?

LADY CHESHIRE
You won't give her away—I see!

BILL
I've told you all there is to tell. We're engaged, we shall be married quietly, and—and—go to Canada.

LADY CHESHIRE
If there weren't more than that to tell you'd be in love with her now.

BILL
I've told you that I am.

LADY CHESHIRE
You are not. [Almost fiercely] I know—I know there's more behind.

BILL
There—is—nothing.

LADY CHESHIRE [Baffled, but unconvinced]
Do you mean that your love for her has been just what it might have been for a lady?

BILL [Bitterly]
Why not?

LADY CHESHIRE [With painful irony]
It is not so as a rule.

BILL
Up to now I've never heard you or the girls say a word against Freda. This isn't the moment to begin, please.

LADY CHESHIRE [Solemnly]
All such marriages end in wretchedness. You haven't a taste or tradition in common. You don't know what marriage is. Day after day, year after year. It's no use being sentimental—for people brought up as we are to have different manners is worse than to have different souls. Besides, it's poverty. Your father will never forgive you, and I've practically nothing. What can you do? You have no profession. How are you going to stand it; with a woman who—? It's the little things.

BILL
I know all that, thanks.

LADY CHESHIRE
Nobody does till they've been through it. Marriage is hard enough when people are of the same class.

[With a sudden movement towards him.

Oh! my dear-before it's too late!

BILL [After a struggle]
It's no good.

LADY CHESHIRE
It's not fair to her. It can only end in her misery.

BILL
Leave that to me, please.

LADY CHESHIRE [With an almost angry vehemence]
Only the very finest can do such things. And you don't even know what trouble's like.

BILL
Drop it, please, mother.

LADY CHESHIRE
Bill, on your word of honour, are you acting of your own free will?

BILL [Breaking away from her]
I can't stand any more.

[He goes out into the workroom.

LADY CHESHIRE
What in God's name shall I do?

[In her distress she walks up and doom the room, then goes to the workroom door, and opens it.

LADY CHESHIRE
Come in here, please, Freda.

[After a seconds pause, **FREDA**, white and trembling, appears in the doorway, followed by **BILL**.

LADY CHESHIRE
No, Bill. I want to speak to her alone.

[**BILL**, does not move.

LADY CHESHIRE [Icily]
I must ask you to leave us.

[**BILL** hesitates; then shrugging his shoulders, he touches **FREDA'S** arms, and goes back into the workroom, closing the door. There is silence.

LADY CHESHIRE
How did it come about?

FREDA
I don't know, my lady.

LADY CHESHIRE
For heaven's sake, child, don't call me that again, whatever happens.

[She walks to the window, and speaks from there.

I know well enough how love comes. I don't blame you. Don't cry. But, you see, it's my eldest son.

[**FREDA** puts her hand to her breast.

Yes, I know. Women always get the worst of these things. That's natural. But it's not only you is it? Does any one guess?

FREDA
No.

LADY CHESHIRE
Not even your father?

[**FREDA** shakes her head.

There's nothing more dreadful than for a woman to hang like a stone round a man's neck. How far has it gone? Tell me!

FREDA
I can't.

LADY CHESHIRE
Come!

FREDA
I—won't.

LADY CHESHIRE [Smiling painfully]
Won't give him away? Both of you the same. What's the use of that with me? Look at me! Wasn't he with you when you went for your holiday this summer?

FREDA
He's—always—behaved—like—a—gentleman.

LADY CHESHIRE
Like a man you mean!

FREDA
It hasn't been his fault! I love him so.

[**LADY CHESHIRE** turns abruptly, and begins to walk up and down the room. Then stopping, she looks intently at **FREDA**.

LADY CHESHIRE
I don't know what to say to you. It's simple madness! It can't, and shan't go on.

FREDA [Sullenly]

I know I'm not his equal, but I am—somebody.

LADY CHESHIRE [Answering this first assertion of rights with a sudden steeliness]
Does he love you now?

FREDA
That's not fair—it's not fair.

LADY CHESHIRE
If men are like gunpowder, Freda, women are not. If you've lost him it's been your own fault.

FREDA
But he does love me, he must. It's only four months.

LADY CHESHIRE [Looking down, and speaking rapidly]
Listen to me. I love my son, but I know him—I know all his kind of man. I've lived with one for thirty years. I know the way their senses work. When they want a thing they must have it, and then—they're sorry.

FREDA [Sullenly]
He's not sorry.

LADY CHESHIRE
Is his love big enough to carry you both over everything?.... You know it isn't.

FREDA
If I were a lady, you wouldn't talk like that.

LADY CHESHIRE
If you were a lady there'd be no trouble before either of you. You'll make him hate you.

FREDA
I won't believe it. I could make him happy—out there.

LADY CHESHIRE
I don't want to be so odious as to say all the things you must know. I only ask you to try and put yourself in our position.

FREDA
Ah, yes!

LADY CHESHIRE
You ought to know me better than to think I'm purely selfish.

FREDA
Would you like to put yourself in my position?

LADY CHESHIRE

What!

FREDA
Yes. Just like Rose.

LADY CHESHIRE [In a low, horror-stricken voice]
Oh!

[There is a dead silence, then going swiftly up to her, she looks straight into **FREDA'S** eyes.

FREDA [Meeting her gaze]
Oh! Yes—it's the truth.

[Then to **BILL** who has come in from the workroom, she gasps out.

I never meant to tell.

BILL
Well, are you satisfied?

LADY CHESHIRE [Below her breath]
This is terrible!

BILL
The Governor had better know.

LADY CHESHIRE
Oh! no; not yet!

BILL
Waiting won't cure it!

[The door from the corridor is thrown open; **CHRISTINE** and **DOT** run in with their copies of the play in their hands; seeing that something is wrong, they stand still. After a look at his mother, **BILL** turns abruptly, and goes back into the workroom. **LADY CHESHIRE** moves towards the window.

JOAN [Following her sisters]
The car's round. What's the matter?

DOT
Shut up!

[**SIR WILLIAM'S** voice is heard from the corridor calling "Dorothy!" As **LADY CHESHIRE**, passing her handkerchief over her face, turns round, he enters. He is in full hunting dress: well-weathered pink, buckskins, and mahogany tops.

SIR WILLIAM
Just off, my dear. [To his **DAUGHTERS**, genially] Rehearsin'? What!

[He goes up to **FREDA** holding out his gloved right hand.

Button that for me, Freda, would you? It's a bit stiff!

[**FREDA** buttons the glove: **LADY CHESHIRE** and the girls watching in hypnotic silence.

SIR WILLIAM
Thank you! "Balmy as May"; scent ought to be first-rate. [To **LADY CHESHIRE**] Good-bye, my dear! Sampson's Gorse—best day of the whole year.

[He pats **JOAN** on the shoulder.

Wish you were cumin' out, Joan.

[He goes out, leaving the door open, and as his footsteps and the chink of his spurs die away, **FREDA** turns and rushes into the workroom.

CHRISTINE
Mother! What—?

[But **LADY CHESHIRE** waves the question aside, passes her **DAUGHTER**, and goes out into the corridor. The sound of a motor car is heard.

JOAN [Running to the window]
They've started—! Chris! What is it? Dot?

DOT
Bill, and her!

JOAN
But what?

DOT [Gloomily]
Heaven knows! Go away, you're not fit for this.

JOAN [Aghast]
I am fit.

DOT
I think not.

JOAN
Chris?

CHRISTINE [In a hard voice]
Mother ought to have told us.

JOAN
It can't be very awful. Freda's so good.

DOT
Call yourself in love, you milk-and-water-kitten!

CHRISTINE
It's horrible, not knowing anything! I wish Runny hadn't gone.

JOAN
Shall I fetch John?

DOT
John!

CHRISTINE
Perhaps Harold knows.

JOAN
He went out with Studdenham.

DOT
It's always like this, women kept in blinkers. Rose-leaves and humbug! That awful old man!

JOAN
Dot!

CHRISTINE
Don't talk of father like that!

DOT
Well, he is! And Bill will be just like him at fifty! Heaven help Freda, whatever she's done! I'd sooner be a private in a German regiment than a woman.

JOAN
Dot, you're awful.

DOT
You-mouse-hearted-linnet!

CHRISTINE
Don't talk that nonsense about women!

DOT
You're married and out of it; and Ronny's not one of these terrific John Bulls.

[To **JOAN** who has opened the door.

Looking for John? No good, my dear; lath and plaster.

JOAN [From the door, in a frightened whisper]
Here's Mabel!

DOT
Heavens, and the waters under the earth!

CHRISTINE
If we only knew!

[**MABEL** comes in, the three girls are silent, with their eyes fixed on their books.

MABEL
The silent company.

DOT [Looking straight at her]
We're chucking it for to-day.

MABEL
What's the matter?

CHRISTINE
Oh! nothing.

DOT
Something's happened.

MABEL
Really! I am sorry. [Hesitating] Is it bad enough for me to go?

CHRISTINE
Oh! no, Mabel!

DOT [Sardonically]
I should think very likely.

[While she is looking from face to face, **BILL** comes in from the workroom. He starts to walk across the room, but stops, and looks stolidly at the four **GIRLS**.

BILL
Exactly! Fact of the matter is, Miss Lanfarne, I'm engaged to my mother's maid.

[No one moves or speaks. Suddenly **MABEL LANFARNE** goes towards him, holding out her hand. **BILL** does not take her hand, but bows. Then after a swift glance at the girls' faces **MABEL** goes out into the corridor, and the three **GIRLS** are left staring at their **BROTHER**.

BILL [Coolly]
Thought you might like to know.

[He, too, goes out into the corridor.

CHRISTINE
Great heavens!

JOAN
How awful!

CHRISTINE
I never thought of anything as bad as that.

JOAN
Oh! Chris! Something must be done!

DOT [Suddenly to herself]
Ha! When Father went up to have his glove buttoned!

[There is a sound, **JACKSON** has come in from the corridor.

JACKSON [To **DOT**]
If you please, Miss, Studdenham's brought up the other two pups. He's just outside. Will you kindly take a look at them, he says?

[There is silence.

DOT [Suddenly]
We can't.

CHRISTINE
Not just now, Jackson.

JACKSON
Is Studdenham and the pups to wait, Mm?

[**DOT** shakes her head violently. But **STUDDENHAM** is seen already standing in the doorway, with a spaniel puppy in either side-pocket. He comes in, and **JACKSON** stands waiting behind him.

STUDDENHAM
This fellow's the best, Miss Dot.

[He protrudes the right-hand pocket.

I was keeping him for my girl—a, proper greedy one—takes after his father.

[The **GIRLS** stare at him in silence.

DOT [Hastily]
Thanks, Studdenham, I see.

STUDDENHAM
I won't take 'em out in here. They're rather bold yet.

CHRISTINE [Desperately]
No, no, of course.

STUDDENHAM
Then you think you'd like him, Miss Dot? The other's got a white chest; she's a lady.

[He protrudes the left-hand pocket.

DOT
Oh, yes! Studdenham; thanks, thanks awfully.

STUDDENHAM
Wonderful faithful creatures; follow you like a woman. You can't shake 'em off anyhow.

[He protrudes the right-hand pocket.

My girl, she'd set her heart on him, but she'll just have to do without.

DOT [As though galvanised]
Oh! no, I can't take it away from her.

STUDDENHAM
Bless you, she won't mind! That's settled, then.

[He turns to the door. To the **PUPPY**.

Ah! would you! Tryin' to wriggle out of it! Regular young limb!

[He goes out, followed by **JACKSON**.

CHRISTINE
How ghastly!

DOT [Suddenly catching sight of the book in her hand]
"Caste!"

[She gives vent to a short sharp laugh.

The curtain falls.

It is five o'clock of the same day. The scene is the smoking-room, with walls of Leander red, covered by old steeplechase and hunting prints. Armchairs encircle a high ferulered hearth, in which a fire is burning. The curtains are not yet drawn across mullioned windows, but electric light is burning. There are two doors, leading, the one to the billiard-room, the other to a corridor. **BILL** is pacing up and doom; **HAROLD**, at the fireplace, stands looking at him with commiseration.

BILL
What's the time?

HAROLD
Nearly five. They won't be in yet, if that's any consolation. Always a tough meet—[softly] as the tiger said when he ate the man.

BILL
By Jove! You're the only person I can stand within a mile of me, Harold.

HAROLD
Old boy! Do you seriously think you're going to make it any better by marrying her?

[**BILL** shrugs his shoulders, still pacing the room.

BILL
Look here! I'm not the sort that finds it easy to say things.

HAROLD
No, old man.

BILL
But I've got a kind of self-respect though you wouldn't think it!

HAROLD
My dear old chap!

BILL
This is about as low-down a thing as one could have done, I suppose—one's own mother's maid; we've known her since she was so high. I see it now that—I've got over the attack.

HAROLD
But, heavens! if you're no longer keen on her, Bill! Do apply your reason, old boy.

[There is silence; while **BILL** again paces up and dozen.

BILL
If you think I care two straws about the morality of the thing.

HAROLD
Oh! my dear old man! Of course not!

BILL
It's simply that I shall feel such a d—d skunk, if I leave her in the lurch, with everybody knowing. Try it yourself; you'd soon see!

HAROLD
Poor old chap!

BILL
It's not as if she'd tried to force me into it. And she's a soft little thing. Why I ever made such a sickening ass of myself, I can't think. I never meant—

HAROLD
No, I know! But, don't do anything rash, Bill; keep your head, old man!

BILL
I don't see what loss I should be, if I did clear out of the country.

[The sound of cannoning billiard balls is heard.

Who's that knocking the balls about?

HAROLD
John, I expect.

[The sound ceases.

BILL
He's coming in here. Can't stand that!

[As **LATTER** appears from the billiard-room, he goes hurriedly out.

LATTER
Was that Bill?

HAROLD
Yes.

LATTER
Well?

HAROLD [Pacing up and down in his turn]
Rat in a cage is a fool to him. This is the sort of thing you read of in books, John! What price your argument with Runny now? Well, it's not too late for you luckily.

LATTER
What do you mean?

HAROLD
You needn't connect yourself with this eccentric family!

LATTER
I'm not a bounder, Harold.

HAROLD
Good!

LATTER
It's terrible for your sisters.

HAROLD
Deuced lucky we haven't a lot of people staying here! Poor mother! John, I feel awfully bad about this. If something isn't done, pretty mess I shall be in.

LATTER
How?

HAROLD
There's no entail. If the Governor cuts Bill off, it'll all come to me.

LATTER
Oh!

HAROLD
Poor old Bill! I say, the play! Nemesis! What? Moral! Caste don't matter. Got us fairly on the hop.

LATTER
It's too bad of Bill. It really is. He's behaved disgracefully.

HAROLD [Warningly]
Well! There are thousands of fellows who'd never dream of sticking to the girl, considering what it means.

LATTER
Perfectly disgusting!

HAROLD
Hang you, John! Haven't you any human sympathy? Don't you know how these things come about? It's like a spark in a straw-yard.

LATTER
One doesn't take lighted pipes into strawyards unless one's an idiot, or worse.

HAROLD
H'm! [With a grin] You're not allowed tobacco. In the good old days no one would hive thought anything of this. My great-grandfather—

LATTER
Spare me your great-grandfather.

HAROLD
I could tell you of at least a dozen men I know who've been through this same business, and got off scot-free; and now because Bill's going to play the game, it'll smash him up.

LATTER
Why didn't he play the game at the beginning?

HAROLD
I can't stand your sort, John. When a thing like this happens, all you can do is to cry out: Why didn't he—? Why didn't she—? What's to be done—that's the point!

LATTER
Of course he'll have to—.

HAROLD
Ha!

LATTER
What do you mean by—that?

HAROLD
Look here, John! You feel in your bones that a marriage'll be hopeless, just as I do, knowing Bill and the girl and everything! Now don't you?

LATTER
The whole thing is—is most unfortunate.

HAROLD
By Jove! I should think it was!

[As he speaks **CHRISTINE** and **KEITH** Come in from the billiard-room. He is still in splashed hunting clothes, and looks exceptionally weathered, thin-lipped, reticent. He lights a cigarette and sinks into an armchair. Behind them **DOT** and **JOAN** have come stealing in.

CHRISTINE
I've told Ronny.

JOAN
This waiting for father to be told is awful.

HAROLD [To **KEITH**]

Where did you leave the old man?

KEITH
Clackenham. He'll be home in ten minutes.

DOT
Mabel's going.

[They all stir, as if at fresh consciousness of discomfiture.

She walked into Gracely and sent herself a telegram.

HAROLD
Phew!

DOT
And we shall say good-bye, as if nothing had happened.

HAROLD
It's up to you, Ronny.

[**KEITH**, looking at **JOAN**, slowly emits smoke; and **LATTER** passing his arm through **JOAN'S**, draws her away with him into the billiard-room.

KEITH
Dot?

DOT
I'm not a squeamy squirrel.

KEITH
Anybody seen the girl since?

DOT
Yes.

HAROLD
Well?

DOT
She's just sitting there.

CHRISTINE [In a hard voice]
As we're all doing.

DOT
She's so soft, that's what's so horrible. If one could only feel—!

KEITH
She's got to face the music like the rest of us.

DOT
Music! Squeaks! Ugh! The whole thing's like a concertina, and some one jigging it!

[They all turn as the door opens, and a **FOOTMAN** enters with a tray of whiskey, gin, lemons, and soda water. In dead silence the **FOOTMAN** puts the tray down.

HAROLD [Forcing his voice]
Did you get a run, Ronny?

[As **KEITH** nods.

What point?

KEITH
Eight mile.

FOOTMAN
Will you take tea, sir?

KEITH
No, thanks, Charles!

[In dead silence again the **FOOTMAN** goes out, and they all look after him.

HAROLD [Below his breath]
Good Gad! That's a squeeze of it!

KEITH
What's our line of country to be?

CHRISTINE
All depends on father.

KEITH
Sir William's between the devil and the deep sea, as it strikes me.

CHRISTINE
He'll simply forbid it utterly, of course.

KEITH
H'm! Hard case! Man who reads family prayers, and lessons on Sunday forbids son to—

CHRISTINE
Ronny!

KEITH
Great Scott! I'm not saying Bill ought to marry her. She's got to stand the racket. But your Dad will have a tough job to take up that position.

DOT
Awfully funny!

CHRISTINE
What on earth d'you mean, Dot?

DOT
Morality in one eye, and your title in the other!

CHRISTINE
Rubbish!

HAROLD
You're all reckoning without your Bill.

KEITH
Ye-es. Sir William can cut him off; no mortal power can help the title going down, if Bill chooses to be such a—

[He draws in his breath with a sharp hiss.

HAROLD
I won't take what Bill ought to have; nor would any of you girls, I should think.

CHRISTINE and **DOT**
Of course not!

KEITH [Patting his wife's arm]
Hardly the point, is it?

DOT
If it wasn't for mother! Freda's just as much of a lady as most girls. Why shouldn't he marry her, and go to Canada? It's what he's really fit for.

HAROLD
Steady on, Dot!

DOT
Well, imagine him in Parliament! That's what he'll come to, if he stays here—jolly for the country!

CHRISTINE
Don't be cynical! We must find a way of stopping Bill.

DOT

Me cynical!

CHRISTINE
Let's go and beg him, Ronny!

KEITH
No earthly! The only hope is in the girl.

DOT
She hasn't the stuff in her!

HAROLD
I say! What price young Dunning! Right about face! Poor old Dad!

CHRISTINE
It's past joking, Harold!

DOT [Gloomily]
Old Studdenham's better than most relations by marriage!

KEITH
Thanks!

CHRISTINE
It's ridiculous—monstrous! It's fantastic!

HAROLD [Holding up his hand]
There's his horse going round. He's in!

[They turn from listening to the sound, to see **LADY CHESHIRE** coming from the billiard-room. She is very pale. They all rise and **DOT** puts an arm round her; while **KEITH** pushes forward his chair. **JOAN** and **LATTER** too have come stealing back.

LADY CHESHIRE
Thank you, Ronny!

[She sits down.

DOT
Mother, you're shivering! Shall I get you a fur?

LADY CHESHIRE
No, thanks, dear!

DOT [In a low voice]
Play up, mother darling!

LADY CHESHIRE [Straightening herself]

What sort of a run, Ronny?

KEITH
Quite fair, M'm. Brazier's to Caffyn's Dyke, good straight line.

LADY CHESHIRE
And the young horse?

KEITH
Carries his ears in your mouth a bit, that's all.

[Putting his hand on her shoulder.

Cheer up, Mem-Sahib!

CHRISTINE
Mother, must anything be said to father? Ronny thinks it all depends on her. Can't you use your influence?

[**LADY CHESHIRE** shakes her head.

CHRISTINE
But, mother, it's desperate.

DOT
Shut up, Chris! Of course mother can't. We simply couldn't beg her to let us off!

CHRISTINE
There must be some way. What do you think in your heart, mother?

DOT
Leave mother alone!

CHRISTINE
It must be faced, now or never.

DOT [In a low voice]
Haven't you any self-respect?

CHRISTINE
We shall be the laughing-stock of the whole county. Oh! mother do speak to her! You know it'll be misery for both of them.

[**LADY CHESHIRE** bows her head.

Well, then?

[**LADY CHESHIRE** shakes her head.

CHRISTINE
Not even for Bill's sake?

DOT
Chris!

CHRISTINE
Well, for heaven's sake, speak to Bill again, mother! We ought all to go on our knees to him.

LADY CHESHIRE
He's with your father now.

HAROLD
Poor old Bill!

CHRISTINE [Passionately]
He didn't think of us! That wretched girl!

LADY CHESHIRE
Chris!

CHRISTINE
There are limits!

LADY CHESHIRE
Not to self-control.

CHRISTINE
No, mother! I can't I never shall—Something must be done! You know what Bill is. He rushes at things so, when he gets his head down. Oh! do try! It's only fair to her, and all of us!

LADY CHESHIRE [Painfully]
There are things one can't do.

CHRISTINE
But it's Bill! I know you can make her give him up, if you'll only say all you can. And, after all, what's coming won't affect her as if she'd been a lady. Only you can do it, mother: Do back me up, all of you! It's the only way!

[Hypnotised by their private longing for what **CHRISTINE** has been urging they have all fixed their eyes on **LADY CHESHIRE**, who looks from, face to face, and moves her hands as if in physical pain.

CHRISTINE [Softly]
Mother!

[**LADY CHESHIRE** suddenly rises, looking towards the billiard-room door, listening. They all follow her eyes. She sits down again, passing her hand over her lips, as **SIR WILLIAM** enters. His hunting clothes are splashed; his face very grim and set. He walks to the fore without a glance at any one, and stands looking down into it. Very quietly, every one but **LADY CHESHIRE** steals away.

LADY CHESHIRE
What have you done?

SIR WILLIAM
You there!

LADY CHESHIRE
Don't keep me in suspense!

SIR WILLIAM
The fool! My God! Dorothy! I didn't think I had a blackguard for a son, who was a fool into the bargain.

LADY CHESHIRE [Rising]
If he were a blackguard he would not be what you call a fool.

SIR WILLIAM [After staring angrily, makes her a slight bow]
Very well!

LADY CHESHIRE [In a low voice]
Bill, don't be harsh. It's all too terrible.

SIR WILLIAM
Sit down, my dear.

[She resumes her seat, and he turns back to the fire.

SIR WILLIAM
In all my life I've never been face to face with a thing like this.

[Gripping the mantelpiece so hard that his hands and arms are seen shaking.

You ask me to be calm. I am trying to be. Be good enough in turn not to take his part against me.

LADY CHESHIRE
Bill!

SIR WILLIAM
I am trying to think. I understand that you've known this—piece of news since this morning. I've known it ten minutes. Give me a little time, please.

[Then, after a silence.

Where's the girl?

LADY CHESHIRE

In the workroom.

SIR WILLIAM [Raising his clenched fist]
What in God's name is he about?

LADY CHESHIRE
What have you said to him?

SIR WILLIAM
Nothing-by a miracle.

[He breaks away from the fire and walks up and down.

My family goes back to the thirteenth century. Nowadays they laugh at that! I don't! Nowadays they laugh at everything—they even laugh at the word lady. I married you, and I don't .... Married his mother's maid! By George! Dorothy! I don't know what we've done to deserve this; it's a death blow! I'm not prepared to sit down and wait for it. By Gad! I am not. [With sudden fierceness] There are plenty in these days who'll be glad enough for this to happen; plenty of these d—d Socialists and Radicals, who'll laugh their souls out over what they haven't the bowels to sees a—tragedy. I say it would be a tragedy; for you, and me, and all of us. You and I were brought up, and we've brought the children up, with certain beliefs, and wants, and habits. A man's past—his traditions—he can't get rid of them. They're—they're himself! [Suddenly] It shan't go on.

LADY CHESHIRE
What's to prevent it?

SIR WILLIAM
I utterly forbid this piece of madness. I'll stop it.

LADY CHESHIRE
But the thing we can't stop.

SIR WILLIAM
Provision must be made.

LADY CHESHIRE
The unwritten law!

SIR WILLIAM
What!

[Suddenly perceiving what she is alluding to.

You're thinking of young—young—[Shortly] I don't see the connection.

LADY CHESHIRE
What's so awful, is that the boy's trying to do what's loyal—and we—his father and mother—!

SIR WILLIAM

I'm not going to see my eldest son ruin his life. I must think this out.

LADY CHESHIRE [Beneath her breath]

I've tried that—it doesn't help.

SIR WILLIAM

This girl, who was born on the estate, had the run of the house—brought up with money earned from me—nothing but kindness from all of us; she's broken the common rules of gratitude and decency—she lured him on, I haven't a doubt!

LADY CHESHIRE [To herself]

In a way, I suppose.

SIR WILLIAM

What! It's ruin. We've always been here. Who the deuce are we if we leave this place? D'you think we could stay? Go out and meet everybody just as if nothing had happened? Good-bye to any prestige, political, social, or anything! This is the sort of business nothing can get over. I've seen it before. As to that other matter—it's soon forgotten—constantly happening—Why, my own grandfather—!

LADY CHESHIRE

Does he help?

SIR WILLIAM [Stares before him in silence-suddenly]

You must go to the girl. She's soft. She'll never hold out against you.

LADY CHESHIRE

I did before I knew what was in front of her—I said all I could. I can't go again now. I can't do it, Bill.

SIR WILLIAM

What are you going to do, then—fold your hands?

[Then as **LADY CHESHIRE** makes a move of distress.

If he marries her, I've done with him. As far as I'm concerned he'll cease to exist. The title—I can't help. My God! Does that meet your wishes?

LADY CHESHIRE [With sudden fire]

You've no right to put such an alternative to me. I'd give ten years of my life to prevent this marriage. I'll go to Bill. I'll beg him on my knees.

SIR WILLIAM

Then why can't you go to the girl? She deserves no consideration. It's not a question of morality: Morality be d—d!

LADY CHESHIRE

But not self-respect....

SIR WILLIAM
What! You're his mother!

LADY CHESHIRE
I've tried; I [putting her hand to her throat] can't get it out.

SIR WILLIAM [Staring at her]

You won't go to her? It's the only chance.

[**LADY CHESHIRE** turns away.

SIR WILLIAM
In the whole course of our married life, Dorothy, I've never known you set yourself up against me. I resent this, I warn you—I resent it. Send the girl to me. I'll do it myself.

[With a look back at him **LADY CHESHIRE** goes out into the corridor.

SIR WILLIAM
This is a nice end to my day!

[He takes a small china cup from of the mantel-piece; it breaks with the pressure of his hand, and falls into the fireplace.

[While he stands looking at it blankly, there is a knock.

SIR WILLIAM
Come in!

[**FREDA** enters from the corridor.

SIR WILLIAM
I've asked you to be good enough to come, in order that—[pointing to chair]—You may sit down.

[But though she advances two or three steps, she does not sit down.

SIR WILLIAM
This is a sad business.

FREDA [Below her breath]
Yes, Sir William.

SIR WILLIAM [Becoming conscious of the depths of feeling before him]
I—er—are you attached to my son?

FREDA [In a whisper] Yes.

SIR WILLIAM

It's very painful to me to have to do this.

[He turns away from her and speaks to the fire.

I sent for you—to—ask—[quickly] How old are you?

FREDA
Twenty-two.

SIR WILLIAM [More resolutely]
Do you expect me to sanction such a mad idea as a marriage?

FREDA
I don't expect anything.

SIR WILLIAM
You know—you haven't earned the right to be considered.

FREDA
Not yet!

SIR WILLIAM
What! That oughtn't to help you! On the contrary. Now brace yourself up, and listen to me!

[She stands waiting to hear her sentence. **SIR WILLIAM** looks at her; and his glance gradually wavers.

SIR WILLIAM
I've not a word to say for my son. He's behaved like a scamp.

FREDA
Oh! no!

SIR WILLIAM [With a silencing gesture]
At the same, time—What made you forget yourself? You've no excuse, you know.

FREDA
No.

SIR WILLIAM
You'll deserve all you'll get. Confound it! To expect me to—It's intolerable! Do you know where my son is?

FREDA [Faintly]
I think he's in the billiard-room with my lady.

SIR WILLIAM [With renewed resolution]
I wanted to—to put it to you—as a—as a—what!

[Seeing her stand so absolutely motionless, looking at him, he turns abruptly, and opens the billiard-room door.

I'll speak to him first. Come in here, please! [To **FREDA**] Go in, and wait!

[**LADY CHESHIRE** and **BILL** come in, and **FREDA** passing them, goes into the billiard-room to wait.

SIR WILLIAM [Speaking with a pause between each sentence]
Your mother and I have spoken of this—calamity. I imagine that even you have some dim perception of the monstrous nature of it. I must tell you this: If you do this mad thing, you fend for yourself. You'll receive nothing from me now or hereafter. I consider that only due to the position our family has always held here. Your brother will take your place. We shall—get on as best we can without you.

[There is a dead silence till he adds sharply.

Well!

BILL
I shall marry her.

LADY CHESHIRE
Oh! Bill! Without love-without anything!

BILL
All right, mother! [To **SIR WILLIAM**] you've mistaken your man, sir. Because I'm a rotter in one way, I'm not necessarily a rotter in all. You put the butt end of the pistol to Dunning's head yesterday, you put the other end to mine to-day. Well!

[He turns round to go out.

Let the d—d thing off!

LADY CHESHIRE
Bill!

BILL [Turning to her]
I'm not going to leave her in the lurch.

SIR WILLIAM
Do me the justice to admit that I have not attempted to persuade you to.

BILL
No! you've chucked me out. I don't see what else you could have done under the circumstances. It's quite all right. But if you wanted me to throw her over, father, you went the wrong way to work, that's all; neither you nor I are very good at seeing consequences.

SIR WILLIAM
Do you realise your position?

BILL [Grimly]
I've a fair notion of it.

SIR WILLIAM [With a sudden outburst]
You have none—not the faintest, brought up as you've been.

BILL
I didn't bring myself up.

SIR WILLIAM [With a movement of uncontrolled anger, to which his son responds]
You—ungrateful young dog!

LATTER
How can you—both?

[They drop their eyes, and stand silent.

SIR WILLIAM [With grimly suppressed emotion]
I am speaking under the stress of very great pain—some consideration is due to me. This is a disaster which I never expected to have to face. It is a matter which I naturally can never hope to forget. I shall carry this down to my death. We shall all of us do that. I have had the misfortune all my life to believe in our position here—to believe that we counted for something—that the country wanted us. I have tried to do my duty by that position. I find in one moment that it is gone—smoke—gone. My philosophy is not equal to that. To countenance this marriage would be unnatural.

BILL
I know. I'm sorry. I've got her into this—I don't see any other way out. It's a bad business for me, father, as well as for you—

[He stops, seeing that **JACKSON** has route in, and is standing there waiting.

JACKSON
Will you speak to Studdenham, Sir William? It's about young Dunning.

[After a moment of dead silence, **SIR WILLIAM** nods, and the butler withdraws.

BILL [Stolidly]
He'd better be told.

SIR WILLIAM
He shall be.

[**STUDDENHAM** enters, and touches his forehead to them all with a comprehensive gesture.

STUDDENHAM
Good evenin', my lady! Evenin', Sir William!

STUDDENHAM
Glad to be able to tell you, the young man's to do the proper thing. Asked me to let you know, Sir William. Banns'll be up next Sunday.

[Struck by the silence, he looks round at all three in turn, and suddenly seeing that **LADY CHESHIRE** is shivering]

Beg pardon, my lady, you're shakin' like a leaf!

BILL [Blurting it out]
I've a painful piece of news for you, Studdenham; I'm engaged to your daughter. We're to be married at once.

STUDDENHAM
I—don't—understand you—sir.

BILL
The fact is, I've behaved badly; but I mean to put it straight.

STUDDENHAM
I'm a little deaf. Did you say—my daughter?

SIR WILLIAM
There's no use mincing matters, Studdenham. It's a thunderbolt—young Dunning's case over again.

STUDDENHAM
I don't rightly follow. She's—You've—! I must see my daughter. Have the goodness to send for her, m'lady.

[**LADY CHESHIRE** goes to the billiard-room, and calls: "FREDA, come here, please."

STUDDENHAM [To **SIR WILLIAM**]
YOU tell me that my daughter's in the position of that girl owing to your son? Men ha' been shot for less.

BILL
If you like to have a pot at me, Studdenham you're welcome.

STUDDENHAM [Averting his eyes from **BILL** at the sheer idiocy of this sequel to his words]
I've been in your service five and twenty years, Sir William; but this is man to man—this is!

SIR WILLIAM
I don't deny that, Studdenham.

STUDDENHAM [With eyes shifting in sheer anger]
No—'twouldn't be very easy. Did I understand him to say that he offers her marriage?

SIR WILLIAM

You did.

STUDDENHAM [Into his beard]
Well—that's something!

[Moving his hands as if wringing the neck of a bird.

I'm tryin' to see the rights o' this.

SIR WILLIAM [Bitterly]
You've all your work cut out for you, Studdenham.

[Again **STUDDENHAM** makes the unconscious wringing movement with his hands.

LADY CHESHIRE [Turning from it with a sort of horror]
Don't, Studdenham! Please!

STUDDENHAM
What's that, m'lady?

LADY CHESHIRE [Under her breath]
Your—your—hands.

[While **STUDDENHAM** is still staring at her, **FREDA** is seen standing in the doorway, like a black ghost.

STUDDENHAM
Come here! You!

[**FREDA** moves a few steps towards her father.

When did you start this?

FREDA [Almost inaudibly]
In the summer, father.

LADY CHESHIRE
Don't be harsh to her!

STUDDENHAM
Harsh!

[His eyes again move from side to side as if pain and anger had bewildered them. Then looking sideways at **FREDA**, but in a gentler voice.

And when did you tell him about—what's come to you?

FREDA
Last night.

STUDDENHAM
Oh! [With sudden menace] You young—!

[He makes a convulsive movement of one hand; then, in the silence, seems to lose grip of his thoughts, and pits his hand up to his head]

I want to clear me mind a bit—I don't see it plain at all.

[Without looking at **BILL**.

'Tis said there's been an offer of marriage?

BILL
I've made it, I stick to it.

STUDDENHAM
Oh! [With slow, puzzled anger] I want time to get the pith o' this. You don't say anything, Sir William?

SIR WILLIAM
The facts are all before you.

STUDDENHAM [Scarcely moving his lips]
M'lady?

[**LADY CHESHIRE** is silent.

STUDDENHAM [Stammering]
My girl was—was good enough for any man. It's not for him that's—that's to look down on her. [To **FREDA**] You hear the handsome offer that's been made you? Well?

[**FREDA** moistens her lips and tries to speak, but cannot.

If nobody's to speak a word, we won't get much forrarder. I'd like for you to say what's in your mind, Sir William.

SIR WILLIAM
I—If my son marries her he'll have to make his own way.

STUDDENHAM [Savagely]
I'm not puttin' thought to that.

SIR WILLIAM
I didn't suppose you were, Studdenham. It appears to rest with your daughter.

[He suddenly takes out his handkerchief, and puts it to his forehead]

Infernal fires they make up here!

[**LADY CHESHIRE**, who is again shivering desperately, as if with intense cold, makes a violent attempt to control her shuddering.

STUDDENHAM [Suddenly]
There's luxuries that's got to be paid for. [To **FREDA**] Speak up, now.

[**FREDA** turns slowly and looks up at **SIR WILLIAM**; he involuntarily raises his hand to his mouth. Her eyes travel on to **LADY CHESHIRE**, who faces her, but so deadly pale that she looks as if she were going to faint. The girl's gaze passes on to **BILL**, standing rigid, with his jaw set.

FREDA
I want—

[Then flinging her arm up over her eyes, she turns from him.

No!

SIR WILLIAM
Ah!

[At that sound of profound relief, **STUDDENHAM**, whose eyes have been following his daughter's, moves towards **SIR WILLIAM**, all his emotion turned into sheer angry pride.

STUDDENHAM
Don't be afraid, Sir William! We want none of you! She'll not force herself where she's not welcome. She may ha' slipped her good name, but she'll keep her proper pride. I'll have no charity marriage in my family.

SIR WILLIAM
Steady, Studdenham!

STUDDENHAM
If the young gentleman has tired of her in three months, as a blind man can see by the looks of him—she's not for him!

BILL [Stepping forward]
I'm ready to make it up to her.

STUDDENHAM
Keep back, there?

[He takes hold of **FREDA**, and looks around him.

Well! She's not the first this has happened to since the world began, an' she won't be the last. Come away, now, come away!

[Taking **FREDA** by the shoulders, he guides her towards the door.

SIR WILLIAM
D—n 'it, Studdenham! Give us credit for something!

STUDDENHAM [Turning his face and eyes lighted up by a sort of smiling snarl]
Ah! I do that, Sir William. But there's things that can't be undone!

[He follows **FREDA** out. As the door closes, **SIR WILLIAM'S** calm gives way. He staggers past his wife, and sinks heavily, as though exhausted, into a chair by the fire. **BILL**, following **FREDA** and **STUDDENHAM**, has stopped at the shut door. **LADY CHESHIRE** moves swiftly close to him. The door of the billiard-room is opened, and **DOT** appears. With a glance round, she crosses quickly to her mother.

DOT [In a low voice]
Mabel's just going, mother! [Almost whispering] Where's Freda? Is it—Has she really had the pluck?

[**LADY CHESHIRE** bending her head for "Yes," goes out into the billiard-room. **DOT** clasps her hands together, and standing there in the middle of the room, looks from her brother to her father, from her father to her brother. A quaint little pitying smile comes on her lips. She gives a faint shrug of her shoulders.

The curtain falls.

John Galsworthy – A Short Biography

John Galsworthy, eldest son of John Galsworthy (1817-1904), a solicitor and company director of Old Jewry, London, and Blanche Bailey (1835-1915), daughter of Charles Bartleet, a needlemaker in Redditch. His father's ancestors originated in Wembury, near Plymouth in England, and Galsworthy, for whom family origins were of significant importance, maintained a close connection with Devon. His more immediate family were considerably wealthy and well established in the shipping industry, and owned a fine estate in Kingston-upon-Thames called Parkfield, where Galsworthy was born on the 14th August 1867. At the age of nine he began education at Saugeen, a Bournemouth preparatory school, before starting at Harrow school in 1881 where he remained until 1886, distinguishing himself as an athlete.

His education at Harrow being successful enough to gain him entrance to Oxford, he began at New College to read law and gained a second-class degree with honours in 1889. Following Lincoln's Inn he was called to the bar in 1890. Despite this recognition he realised that he was not keen to actually begin practising law and so he resolved instead to look after the family's shipping business while specialising himself in Marine Law. This decision saw him take to the seas to destinations such as Vancouver, Island and South AFrica, though it was at the age of twenty-five on one particular journey to Australia, motivated by an (unfulfilled) intention to meet Robert Louis Stevenson on Samoa that he would being to realise fully his literary interests: though he was not considering becoming a writer at this time, his enjoyment of literature was enough to encourage an attempt at meeting a great writer and eventually enabled one of the most significant encounters of his life. He made the journey with his friend Edward Sanderson and, though he missed Stevenson, he met Joseph Conrad, a fellow future author famed for his novels which were often nautically themed. At the time Conrad was the first mate of the sailing-ship

Torrens moored in the harbour of Adelaide, Australia; still very much focused on his ship-borne career, he was yet to begin his writing in earnest.

Indeed, though neither knew at the time, both Conrad and Galsworthy were at similar junctures in their lives, their time spent as sea acting as a transitional period during which each found their literary calling. It is perhaps owning to this unknown common ground that they became close friends. During his time on the Torrens Galsworthy recorded several details, offering a frank and valuable characterisation of Conrad while also illuminating his own experiences as a student of Marine Law.

"I supposed to be studying navigation for the Admiralty Bar, would every day work out the position of the ship with the captain. On one side of the saloon table we would sit and check our observations with those of Conrad, who from the other side of the table would look at us a little quizzically."

On his return to England and the cessation of his nautical voyaging, Galsworthy began an affair with the wife of his first cousin, Major Arthur John Galsworthy. Ada Nemesis Pearson Cooper (1864-1956), the daughter of Emanuel Copper, an obstetrician from Norwich, remained married to the Major for ten years and the affair remained secret for its duration. In order to conceal the affair they took considerable pains to avoid suspicion. One such tactic was to stay in a secluded farmhouse called Wingstone in the village on Manaton on Dartmoor, in Devon. In Galsworthy's decision to choose Devon as the location for their clandestine rendezvous we see evidence of Galsworthy's affection for the place of his father's origin. It was only when, in 1905, she divorced the Major that their affair became known following their marriage on 23rd September of that year.

Galsworthy now took to writing sometime after having met Conrad and his career began in earnest when, in 1897, his first work, From the Four Winds, a volume of short stories, was published under the pseudonym John Sinjohn. He succeeded this in 1898 with Jocelyn, his first novel, and then his second in 1900, Villa Rubein. In 1901 he published a second volume of short stories, A Man of Devon, which was the last of his work to be published under pseudonym. The first of his work to be published under his own name was The Island Pharisees in 1904, a novel of social observation, seasoned with flashes of satire and propaganda. His decision to write under his own name is arguably owing to the recent death of his father, either as a mark of respect to his name or because now he was able to publish freely without incurring the possibility of paternal disappointment at his choice of career. It also marked a shift in his professionalism; he had hitherto published with small, independent publishers, but The Island Pharisees was published by Heinemann, a far more established House and one with whom he remained for the duration of his writing career.

He arguably cemented his position and maturity as a writer when, in 1906, he saw the publication of both his first major play, The Silver Box, and the novel The Man of Property. Each was published to considerable critical acclaim, and to achieve both in such a short space of time was impressive. the Silver Box concerns the imbalance in the justice system with regards to criminals of differing class by contrasting the treatment of a poor thief and a rich thief, both of whom stole silver cigarette cases but for very different reasons. The complexity of individual experience when not dealt with in public is highlighted and questioned in a bravely critical manner; despite the clear issues it raises with class and privilege, the final night was attended by the Price and Princess of Wales. The Man of Property was the first novel in the famous The Forsyte Saga, a trilogy of novels with an 'interlude' between each one, written between 1906 and 1921. Dealing with the questions of status, class and materialism, The Man of Property introduces us to the Forsyte family, particularly Soames Forsyte, who is acutely aware of his status as 'new money' and equally keen to assert himself as a wealthy man. Jealous of his wife and desperate to own things in order to confirm his wealth to those observing him, he engineers a plan to keep his wife from her friends which backfires spectacularly when, instead of cutting her off, all Soames achieves is enabling her to have an affair. This drives Soames to terrible actions with terrible consequences, which Galsworthy depicts with confidence.

Very typically Edwardian, the novel focuses on conflict between property and art, and to a certain degree much of its emotional power is drawn from Galsworthy's own life, particularly his affair with Ada. Their rendezvous in the countryside of Devon mirror the manner in which Forsyte seeks to relocate his wife and; though theirs was a much healthier relationship, there are clear similarities. By examining the fragile nature of the class system and those moving within it Galsworthy offered an important perspective on the relationships between material wealth, personal happiness and obsession, and the manner in which these change over time. His contemporaries widely regarded the publication of this novel as marking the end of Victorianism. His friend Conrad praised it as "indubitably a piece of art" and, though the notoriously risqué D.H. Lawrence lamented the novel's timidity in the face of sexuality and sensuality, he considered it potentially "a very great novel, a very great satire".

Though he continued to write both plays and novels, it was his work as a playwright for which he was most celebrated by his contemporaries. Indeed, his next novel, The Country House, seems uncharacteristically unfocused, its satirical view of those belonging to the country set comparatively unremarkable and weakly characterised, while at times the tone of satire becomes one of ironic detachment. In 1909 he published Fraternity, an exploration of of the various connections between urban society and the social classes therein, though its representation of lower-class Londoners is utterly unconvincing and ill-informed. Remaining with the subject of the landed gentry and the society surrounding it, in 1915 he published The Freelands, which does not stray far from conservative discussions of capitalism, the rural economy and their interrelationship.

His drama, however, featured a convincingly muted realism, directed at a relatively small, educated and politically-aware audience. His social agenda is prevalent here too, and is represented in a simple and static manner producing arresting instances of high drama. This talent for creating moments of captivating theatre is complimented by an instinctual sense of balance enabling his narratives to vacillate between their emotional high- and low-points, ultimately reaching conclusive equilibrium. This is particularly evident in one of his most popular plays, Strife, published in 1909 and examining the antagonists in a strike at a Cornish tin mine. In this, and in 1910's Justice, he approaches his subject with sympathy, irony and balance, which establishes a position of narrative authority while garnering the audiences trust that he is representing his characters and their motives justly. Justice condemns the use of solitary confinement in prisons, a reformist agenda which caught the liberality of his contemporary audiences along with the home secretary, Winston Churchill. Despite he was careful to disassociate himself with politics and professed himself apolitical, he and his work were nevertheless aligned with the views of the Liberal establishment. He spent much of the duration of the First World War working in a field hospital in France as an orderly having been passed over for military service.

Despite the popularity and brilliance of his work, it was only in 1920 that he had his first true commercial success with The Skin Game, a melodrama dealing with ethics, property and class. The play was adapted by Alfred Hitchcock in 1931. Galsworthy, meanwhile, had turned down a knighthood in 1918, considering his work not sufficient to be made a knight of the realm. He did, however, accept the Belgian Palmes d'Or in the following year. In 1920 he published the second novel in the Forsyte Saga, In Chancery, in which he resumes many of the themes of the first novel, focusing on the marital disharmony between Soames Forsyte and his wife. Katherine Mansfield considered it "a fascinating, brilliant book" in her review in The Atheneum. Then, in 1921, he was elected as the PEN International Literary Club's first president. The concluding novel to The Forsyte Saga, To Let was published in 1921 with a kind of peace being found between Forsyte and his now-ex wife, though he is left contemplating his losses and his greed. More ironic treatment of class confusions followed in Loyalties, bringing with it more popular success which lasted until 1926 and Escape, the last of his popular plays. Though he enjoyed popular success it was inconsistent and relatively small. His Collected Plays was published in 1929.

Over the course of time the appreciation of his work has gradually shifted from his plays to his novels, and particularly the detail and intricacy of his chronicle of English social difference, tension and pretension in The Forsyte Saga. Its success encouraged Galsworthy to revisit Soames Forsyte in a second trilogy, A Modern Comedy, which follows Soames's obsessive love of his daughter Fleur. In its three volumes, The White Monkey (1924), The Silver Spoon (1936) and Swan Song (1928) he examines the English commercial upper-middle class and its ideologies, its instinct to possess as its only way of distinguishing itself manifested in the poisonous materialism of Soames. Interestingly, this emergent social class which he so vehemently criticises is the very class from which he emerged. He witnessed first-hand its insularity, its chauvinism, its restrictive and oppressive morality, its stubborn imperialism and its materialism, and it is this experience which enables him to write so comfortably about it. Swan Song is widely considered among the best of Galsworthy's writing for the depth of its exploration of society and its heightened emotional subtlety. In 1929 he was appointed to the Order of Merit, despite having turned down a knighthood earlier. He spent his last years writing a third trilogy, End of the Chapter, beginning in 1931 with Maid in Waiting, Flowering Wilderness in 1932 and concluding with Over The River in 1933. These are significantly less coherent works and are indicative of his deteriorating health. Indeed, in 1932 he was awarded the Nobel Prize, though he was too ill to attend the ceremony.

Throughout the course of his career he received honorary degrees from the universities of St Andrews (1922), Manchester (1927), Dublin (1929), Cambridge (1930), Sheffield (1930), Oxford (1931), and Princeton (1931). In 1926 New College, Oxford, elected him as an honourary fellow. In photographs he is portrayed as handsome, fastidiously dressed and dignified. He was unusually compassionate and this saw him involved in several charitable and humane causes throughout the course of his life, including penal reforms, attacks on theatrical censorship and campaigning for animal rights. Though he spent the majority of the final seven years of his life at his home in Bury, West Sussex, it was at his home in Hampstead, London, that he died of a brain tumour on 31st January, 1933, six weeks after having been too ill to attend the ceremony in honour of his receiving the Nobel Prize. According to demands made in his will he was cremated and his ashes scattered over the South Downs from an aeroplane. Also in his will was his wish to leave cottages to several of his astonished tenants. He is memorialised in Highgate 'New' Cemetery and in the cloisters of New College, Oxford, where he was an honourary fellow.

John Galsworthy – A Concise Bibliography

From the Four Winds, 1897 (as John Sinjohn)
Jocelyn, 1898 (as John Sinjohn)
Villa Rubein, 1900 (as John Sinjohn)
A Man of Devon, 1901 (as John Sinjohn)
The Island Pharisees, 1904
The Silver Box, 1906 (his first play)
The Man of Property, 1906 – First book of The Forsyte Saga (1922)

The Silver Spoon, 1926 – Second book of A Modern Comedy
Verses New and Old, 1926
Castles in Spain, 1927
A Silent Wooing, 1927 – First Interlude of A Modern Comedy
Passers By, 1927 – Second Interlude of A Modern Comedy
Swan Song, 1928 – Third book of A Modern Comedy
The Manaton Edition, 1923–26 (collection, 30 vols.)
Exiled, 1929
The Roof, 1929
On Forsyte 'Change, 1930
Two Essays on Conrad, 1930
Soames and the Flag, 1930
The Creation of Character in Literature, 1931 (The Romanes Lecture for 1931).
Maid in Waiting, 1931 – First book of End of the Chapter (1934)
Forty Poems, 1932
Flowering Wilderness, 1932 – Second book of End of the Chapter
Autobiographical Letters of Galsworthy: A Correspondence with Frank Harris, 1933
One More River (originally Over the River), 1933 – Third book of End of the Chapter
The Grove Edition, 1927–34 (collection, 27 Vols.)
Collected Poems, 1934
Punch and Go, 1935
The Life and Letters, 1935
The Winter Garden, 1935
Forsytes, Pendyces and Others, 1935
Selected Short Stories, 1935
Glimpses and Reflections, 1937